JENNIFER DEAN

5 Minute Daily Devos for Kids

What's the Buzz on the Bee-Atitudes?

First edition

ISBN: 978-1-0690801-2-7

This book was professionally typeset on Reedsy.
Find out more at reedsy.com

HUGE thanks to Jesus for enabling me to write this mini-devotional for His glory.

This book is dedicated to my four beautiful children— Israel, Ezekiel, Benjamin, and Eliyanah. You continue to teach me about the love of our Heavenly Father and how to live out the Beatitudes in my everyday life. You are my greatest blessings!

Contents

Introduction

Hey There, Busy Bees!

We're absolutely buzzing with excitement that you've decided to join us on this thrilling Bible adventure to uncover the sweet secrets of the beatitudes Jesus taught!

I'm Jen, your guide on this fun journey, and I've whipped up this mini-devotional just for you. It's a true delight and privilege to journey with you as we dive into God's Word over the next 14 days.

Think of this devotional as a turbo-charged snack for your soul—just 5 minutes a day to sprinkle into your routine! My hope is that this time will refresh your spirit, encourage your heart, and pull you closer to God. Each day, we'll shine a spotlight on a beatitude from Matthew 5:3-12, amongst other Bible verses, and we will explore how to cultivate these amazing qualities in our lives.

Here's the fun stuff you can look forward to:

Key Verse: We'll kick things off with a Bible verse that highlights the beatitude we're focusing on for the day.

Heart-to-Heart Sharing: I'll spill some personal stories, lessons, and golden nuggets of encouragement to help you weave these truths into your daily life.

Scripture Memorization: Over the next two weeks, we'll tackle memorizing Matthew 5:3-12 together, along with a few more Bible verses sprinkled in the mix. By the end, you'll have these powerful Bible verses locked in your mind, ready to turbocharge your walk with God!

Activity: At the end of each devotional we will share a small activity you can do to help lock in the truth we've learned that day!

I'm so pumped for the surprises awaiting us during this time! So grab your Bible, snuggle up in a cozy nook, and let's plunge into God's Word together. I'm sure these next 14 days will be a whirlwind of transformation, and we can't wait to see how God shakes things up in our lives!

Let's dive in and discover what the Beatitude buzz is all about!

Day 1 - What's the Buzz on the Beatitudes?

Matthew 5:3
Blessed are the poor in spirit,
for theirs is the kingdom of heaven.

Hi, friends!

Welcome to Day 1 of our Bible adventure! Let's kick things off by unraveling the mystery of the Beatitudes! Have you ever heard of Matthew 5? It's also known as Jesus' "Sermon on the Mount," where He literally spilled the beans from a mountain in Israel!

Now, "Beatitudes" (bee-at-i-tudes) might sound fancy, but it simply hails from the Latin "beatus," meaning "blessed" or "super-duper happy!" So, what's the deal with being "blessed"? It's realizing that every goodie in life comes from Jesus, and we're blessed to know and be loved by Him.

When Jesus first shared these beatitudes, it was like He was speaking in riddles to the crowd that followed Him. But fear not! For the next 14 days, we'll unpack these gems to deepen our friendship with Jesus and learn how to shine like stars in this sometimes wobbly world by embracing His wisdom from the Sermon on the Mount. Buckle up, because these words will challenge us and humble our hearts as we recognize just how much we need Him!

So, what's the buzz all about? Stay tuned for tomorrow as we dive headfirst into the very first beatitude!

Prayer:
Jesus, over the next 14 days, help me unlock the treasures in the Beatitudes. As I grow closer to You, guide me to share Your truths with everyone around me. In Your holy, amazing, awesome name, Jesus, amen.

Memorize:
Ready to kick off Day 1? Let's memorize Matthew 5:3.
Matthew 5:3
Blessed are the poor in spirit,
for theirs is the kingdom of heaven.

Activity:
Draw a treasure chest below and fill it with things that make you feel rich in spirit- like love, kindness, and joy. Discuss how these treasures are more valuable than money!

Day 2 - What's the Buzz on Being Poor in Spirit?

Matthew 5:3
Blessed are the poor in spirit,
for theirs is the kingdom of heaven.

What does it mean to be "poor in spirit"? Does it mean we're walking around with frowns glued to our faces and joy is on vacation? Nope! Being poor in spirit is all about realizing we need a little divine assistance from Jesus in our lives. It's like admitting we can't ace every test on our own and that we need God's help—like a trusty sidekick!

Picture this: trying to tackle a brand-new video game without peeking at the instructions or having a buddy show you the ropes. Chaos and frustration would reign supreme, right? That's what life feels like without God's guidance—like wandering in a maze with no exit! But when we say, "Hey, I need you, Jesus!" we unlock the ultimate cheat code for life. Jesus tells us that being "poor in spirit" means we get VIP access to His kingdom!

What a fantastic deal—trust in Him, and you get to join the coolest family ever- God's!

Prayer:
Jesus, I'm waving my flag of need! I need Your forgiveness, grace, and love. Thanks for making my heart Your cozy home when I humble myself before You. Help me to live for You every single day! Amen.

Daily Memory Verse:
Alright, busy bees, let's buzz through **Matthew 5:3** today by memory!
Matthew 5:3
Blessed are the poor in spirit,
for theirs is the kingdom of heaven.

Activity:
What are some areas in your life where you need God's help? Do you sometimes try to do things all on your own without asking God or others for help? Let's make a fun list below of ways we depend on God every single day.

Day 3 - What's the Buzz on Those Who Mourn?

Matthew 5: 4
Blessed are those who mourn,
for they will be comforted.

Have you ever felt your heart do a little tango with sadness? Maybe a buddy packed up and moved, you lost your furry friend or life just decided to throw a curve ball! Mourning is that heavy feeling of grief, but guess what? Jesus swoops in with a comforting twist, saying we're blessed even when the clouds roll in. Why? Because God's got our backs and promises to wrap us in a cozy blanket of comfort at all times!

Imagine this: you take a tumble and scrape your knee, and your loving parent or someone that loves you rushes in with a warm hug to make it all better. That's God for you! He's got a deep sense for our heartaches and is always ready to embrace us with peace. Sometimes His comfort comes through the sweet gestures of friends, family, or even that one teacher who knows just how to brighten your day. Other times, it's a direct line to our hearts when we pray or think about His promises.

Jesus wants us to keep in mind that even when life feels like a stormy rollercoaster, we can trust that God sees our tears and hears our sighs. He's our ultimate cheerleader, always there to help us through the tough times!

Prayer:
Lord Jesus, please comfort me when I feel sad or lonely. Thank You for always being near to me at all times, especially when life can feel like a stormy rollercoaster. Amen.

Daily Memory Verse:
Let's try some actions to help us memorize this Bible verse today. Get creative!
Matthew 5:4
Blessed are those who mourn,
for they will be comforted.

Activity:
Create a "Comfort Jar" filled with notes of encouragement for friends who might be feeling sad. Share how helping others can bring happiness.

Day 4 - What's the Buzz on Being Meek?

Matthew 5:5
Blessed are the meek,
for they will inherit the earth.

Being meek means being gentle and humble. It doesn't mean being weak or letting people walk all over you. Instead, it's about showing kindness, patience, and not always needing to be in control or get your way. Jesus says that people who are meek will inherit the earth! That means God will bless them with great things because of their gentle and humble hearts.

Think of a soft breeze on a warm day. It's gentle, but it can make you feel so good and bring relief. Meekness is like that—it's quiet, but it can make a big difference. Jesus was the best example of meekness. Even though He had all the power in the world, He chose to be kind and gentle with people, even when they didn't treat Him kindly.

When we choose to be meek, we show others what God's love looks like. We don't need to be the loudest, strongest, or most powerful to make an impact. Instead, our gentleness and patience can touch people's hearts in ways we might not even realize.

Prayer:

Dear Jesus, please help me to be humble and kind, not wanting my own way all the time. Thank You that You were the ultimate example of what it means to be meek. Help me to be more like You, Jesus. Amen.

Daily Memory Verse:

Let's try to act out this Bible verse today to help us lock it into our memory vaults!

Matthew 5:5

Blessed are the meek,

for they will inherit the earth.

Activity:

Play a game where everyone takes turns being "meek" (gentle) while trying to balance a book on their head. Talk about how being gentle can make us strong.

Day 5 - What's the Buzz on Being Hungry and Thirsty for Righteousness?

Matthew 5:6
Blessed are those who hunger and thirst for righteousness, for they will be filled.

Have you ever been really hungry or thirsty after playing outside or after a long day? When you're hungry or thirsty, all you can think about is getting food or water. Jesus uses this example to explain what it means to "hunger and thirst for righteousness." Righteousness means doing what is right and living in a way that pleases God.

Just like we crave food when we're hungry, we should desire to live a life that honours God. When we seek to do what is right, to be kind, and to live the way Jesus taught us, God promises to fill us. This doesn't mean He'll give us physical food, but He will fill our hearts with joy, peace, and His love.

We can "hunger and thirst" for righteousness by praying, reading the Bible, and asking God to help us make good choices every single day. When we do these things, God will help us grow and be more like Jesus every day.

Prayer:
Jesus, Thank You that You're right there to fill me up when I'm in need. Please help me to want what is right and good. Fill my heart with love for You and others. In Your amazing name, Jesus, amen.

Daily Memory Verse:
Let's act this Bible verse out today, friends. Say it loud and clear as you act it out!

Matthew 5:6
Blessed are those who hunger and thirst for righteousness,
for they will be filled."

Activity:
Make "Righteousness Smoothies" using healthy ingredients. Discuss what it means to seek goodness in our lives like we seek food and drink to nourish our bodies.

Day 6 - What's the Buzz on Being Merciful?

Matthew 5:7
Blessed are the merciful,
for they will be shown mercy.

Hey, fantastic friends!

Today, we're diving into the glittery pool of mercy! So, what's the buzz on mercy? It's all about dishing out kindness and forgiveness, even when someone totally doesn't deserve it. Jesus spills the beans that when we sprinkle mercy on others, God showers us with it right back! Amazing!

Remember that time someone gave you a free pass after you totally messed up? Feels like winning the lottery, right? Jesus is all about that mercy life! He forgives our sins and hands us a shiny do-over whenever we need it. Being merciful means letting go of grudges, being sweet to the sourpusses, and lending a helping hand—even when it feels like climbing a mountain.

Sure, it can be a tough cookie to chew, but when we embrace mercy, we're spreading the warm fuzzies of Jesus' love all around! Plus, God's got our backs—He promises that when we're merciful, He'll shower us with mercy, too! How awesome is that?

Prayer:
Jesus, please help me to forgive others and show kindness, just like You do for me. Help me to show mercy even when it's hard. Thank You, Jesus. Amen.

Daily Memory Verse:
Let's try whispering this Bible quietly at first. Say it 3 times quietly. On the fourth time, say it as loud as you can!
Matthew 5:7
Blessed are the merciful,
for they will be shown mercy.

Activity:
Write down acts of kindness below that you can do this week. Share them with your family and encourage everyone to complete their list.

Day 7 - What's the Buzz on Being Pure in Heart?

Matthew 5:8
Blessed are the pure in heart,
for they will see God.

So, what's the scoop on rocking a pure heart? Having a pure heart means our love radar is tuned to God and we're all about doing what's right. It's like decluttering your mind of all those pesky bad thoughts and ditching the wrongdoings. Jesus even spills the tea that with pure hearts, we get a VIP pass to see God! WOW! How cool is that?!

Imagine a sparkling clean window—so clear you can see the world outside! But when it's smudged with fingerprints, it's hard to get a clear view. Our hearts are just like that window. Keep them clean and pure, and voilà! You'll see God's love shining through and hear His voice ringing in your ears.

Now, don't get it twisted—having a pure heart doesn't mean you're perfect, just that you're trying your best to live in a way that gives God a high-five. Need a little help keeping that heart of yours shiny? Just pray, dive into His Word, and steer clear of the stuff that tries to pull you away from doing what He says is right!

Prayer:
God, please help me to keep my heart clean from wrong thoughts and actions. Please help me to love You above everything else. In Jesus' name, amen.

Daily Memory Verse:
Today, as you memorize this beautiful Bible verse let's make a heart shape with our hands and say the Bible verse out loud.
Matthew 5:8
Blessed are the pure in heart,
for they will see God.

Activity:
Create a "Pure Heart" collage below using magazine cutouts that represent purity and goodness. Talk about how our hearts can shine brightly for Jesus every single day.

Day 8 - What's the Buzz on Being Peacemakers?

Matthew 5:9
Blessed are the peacemakers,
for they will be called children of God.

So, what's the buzz on being a peacemaker? It's all about sprinkling peace like confetti instead of stirring the pot! Jesus absolutely beams when we help others play nice, promising that peace-bringers are His besties. How cool is that?

Picture a time when you witnessed a showdown—arguments flying like popcorn! It's tempting to jump into the fray or pick a side. But hold on! Jesus wants us to don our superhero capes and be peacemakers, helping everyone chill out and harmonize. When we spread peace, we're basically delivering a slice of God's love to those around us. We can do this by using kind words, helping siblings settle their squabbles, and choosing not to throw shade ourselves.

And let's not forget, Jesus is the grandmaster of peace! He bridged the gap between us and God by taking one for the team on the cross. When we follow His example, we show that we are His children, part of God's family!

Prayer:

Jesus, please help me follow Your example by being a peacemaker, bringing kindness and peace to others- especially when I feel like fighting, too. Amen.

Daily Memory Verse:

Today as we memorize this Bible verse let's make a fun "peace" sign with our hands to remind us that we are called to be peacemakers, friends.

Matthew 5:9

Blessed are the peacemakers,

for they will be called children of God.

Activity:

Play a team-building game that requires cooperation and communication. Discuss how peacemakers work together to create harmony.

Day 9 - What's the Buzz on Being Persecuted?

Matthew 5:10
Blessed are those who are persecuted because of righteousness, for theirs is the kingdom of heaven.

Alright, friends! Let's break down this hefty word "persecuted" — it's like a fancy way of saying people aren't being too nice just because you're following Jesus. Sometimes, people scratch their heads at our faith and decide to poke fun or treat us unfairly. But guess what? Jesus totally gets it; He faced extremely mean treatment, even though He was the epitome of perfection and kindness. When the teasing gets tough, Jesus gives us a high-five and says we're blessed!

Persecution can show up in all sorts of ways—maybe it's a classmate throwing shade at school for your beliefs, or folks who just can't handle a good Jesus chat. But here's the bright side: when we stand tall for what's right, God's kingdom is just around the corner, waiting for us! He sees our bravery and love, and oh boy, does He have some rewards lined up!

Facing persecution isn't exactly a walk in the park, but take heart! Jesus is right there beside us, ready to pump us up with strength and courage whenever we need it. Let's keep shining no matter the cost!

Prayer:

Jesus, help me to be brave when people don't understand my faith in You. Thank You for promising me Your kingdom and for always being super close. Amen.

Daily Memory Verse:

Let's rally and say this Bible verse out loud! The more times we say it the better we will commit it to our memory banks.

Matthew 5:10

Blessed are those who are persecuted because of righteousness, for theirs is the kingdom of heaven.

Activity:

Share stories of courageous characters from the Bible and modern day history who were persecuted for their faith in Jesus. Talk about standing up for what is right, even when it's tough. Also, take some time to make a list below of friends and family you can pray for and share Jesus with in practical ways in the upcoming days.

Day 10 - What's the Buzz on Being Insulted for Jesus?

Matthew 5:11
Blessed are you when people insult you, persecute you and falsely say all kinds of evil against you because of Me.

Hey, friends! Have you ever had someone poke fun at your faith in Jesus? Yikes, right? It's a bummer, but guess what? Jesus totally gets it! He dealt with all sorts of insults and unfairness, and He never did anything wrong! In fact, He assures us that when we're treated poorly for sticking by Him, we're actually wearing a badge of blessing!

Sure, facing laughter or jabs about our beliefs can feel like climbing a mountain in flip-flops, but we can take a cozy little comfort knowing we're standing tall for what's right. Jesus is fist-pumping us when we hold strong, even if others are scratching their heads.

So, remember this: as we follow Jesus, we've got a trusty sidekick! He's right there with us on this wild ride, and He promises a glorious reward for our faithfulness in the end. Keep shining bright!

Prayer:

Jesus, please help me to be strong when others make fun of me for loving You. I know You are always with me. Thank You so much, amen.

Daily Memory Verse:

We've shortened the Bible memory verse (below) today to help it be easier to memorize. Let's say it out loud 5 times.

Matthew 5:11

Blessed are you when people insult you because of Me.

Activity:

Create joyful reaction faces on paper plates and then role-play situations where we might face negativity but choose joy instead.

Day 11 - What's the Buzz on Rejoicing?

Matthew 5:12
Rejoice and be glad,
because great is your reward in heaven.

Even when life is hard, Jesus tells us to rejoice and be glad! How can we do that when we're going through tough times or being bullied for loving Jesus? The answer is that we can be happy because we know something amazing is waiting for us in heaven! Jesus promises that when we live for Him, even when it's hard, we will be rewarded. Amazing!

Imagine you're running a long race. It's tiring and tough, but you know that at the end there's a big prize waiting for you. That's how it is with our faith in Jesus. Even though we face challenges and struggles now, we can keep going because we know God has something wonderful waiting for us in heaven.

So when you feel discouraged or face hard times, remember to rejoice and worship Him! Jesus sees everything you're going through, and He has a reward ready for you in heaven.

Prayer:

Dear Jesus, help me to rejoice in You, even when things are hard, because I know You have a reward waiting for me in heaven. Thank you for caring about me. Amen.

Daily Memory Verse:

With big, amazing smiles on our faces let's say this Bible memory verse 5 times together out loud.

Matthew 5:12

Rejoice and be glad,

because great is your reward in heaven.

Activity:

Spend time thanking God for the blessings in your life. Journal a prayer or draw a picture below expressing gratitude for each Beatitude you've learned about.

Day 12 - The Bee-Atitudes as a Picture of Jesus

P hilippians 2:5
In your relationships with one another,
have the same mindset as Christ Jesus.

Friends, the Beatitudes aren't just a cheeky list of rules—they're basically a snapshot of Jesus in action! He's the ultimate role model, embodying all that goodness: humble, kind, merciful, and a peacemaker. His time on earth was like a masterclass in serving others and giving God a high-five!

When we decide to follow Jesus, it's like getting a heavenly makeover! We might not hit perfection every day, but we can totally flex our love, kindness, mercy, and humility muscles. The more we hang out with Jesus through prayer and diving into the Bible, the more we'll start thinking and acting like Him—how cool is that?

Jesus wants us to rock His mindset, which means putting others first, forgiving those who step on our toes, and making the right choices, even when it feels like climbing Mount Everest!

Prayer:

Jesus, help me to live like You, loving others and being humble in everything I do. I know it will be hard at times but with Your help, I know it's possible. Thank you for loving me just as I am! Amen.

Daily Memory Verse:

Today we've shortened the Bible memory verse to help us commit the main point of the scripture in our memory banks. Let's say it as loud as we can 5 times, friends!

Philippians 2:5

Have the same mindset as Christ Jesus.

Activity:

Think about one Beatitude that stands out to you. How can you share this blessing with others? Journal a short letter or draw a picture below to share your thoughts.

Day 13 - What's the Buzz on Living the Beatitudes?

Revelation 22:12
Look, I am coming soon! My reward is with me, and I will give to each person according to what they have done."

Friends, Jesus is throwing down the ultimate promise: He's coming back, and when He does, he's got a treasure chest of rewards for all His followers!

Sure, living out those Beatitudes can feel like climbing a mountain sometimes, but Jesus gives us a nudge, reminding us it's totally worth the trek! He's got eyes like a hawk on our faithful shenanigans, and trust me, He's taking notes for the big reward ceremony!

But hold onto your horses, because these rewards aren't just earthly goodies! The grand prize? An eternity of amazingness with Jesus in heaven! We can't wait for that day when He returns, beaming with joy for all our good deeds.

So let's keep our peepers glued to that heavenly reward and strut through each day honouring Him like the rock stars we are!

Prayer:
Jesus, thank You for promising us great rewards in heaven. Help me live for You every single day. Amen.

Daily Memory Verse:
This is a long Bible verse today friends but we can do it! Let's act it out and say it out loud as we do. Act it out a few times, this will help us lock it into our memory.
Revelation 22:12
Look, I am coming soon! My reward is with me,
and I will give to each person according to what they have done.

Activity:
Write a short story or comic strip below featuring people who live out one of the Beatitudes. Share your stories with your family and friends.

Day 14 - What's the Buzz on Living It Out?

J ames 1:22
Do not merely listen to the Word, and so deceive yourselves.
Do what it says.

Day 14! Can you believe it? You've nailed this mini Bible study on the Beatitudes like a pro! Now, let's sprinkle some wisdom on our final devotional about bringing those beatitudes to life!

Reading about the Beatitudes is like flipping through a menu—delicious, but we need to take a bite! The Good Book, the Bible, wants us to be "doers" of God's Word, not just couch potatoes munching on knowledge. It's all about practicing what we've learned every single day!

When we soak in Jesus' teachings on the Beatitudes, let's ask ourselves: How can I sprinkle a little mercy today? How can I be the ultimate peacemaker with my siblings? What does it mean to crave righteousness? These are the golden questions to ponder each day!

Living out the Beatitudes is all about putting others first, spreading love like confetti, and strutting our stuff the way Jesus did. When we embrace this, we shine a light on what it means to follow Him, and trust me, it's like a magnet that draws people closer to Jesus!

Prayer:
Lord Jesus, please help me to live out the Beatitudes, and to not just listen, but to do what You ask every single day. Thank You so much for your mercy, grace and strength to do what is right even when others are not looking. Thank You for Who You are. Amen.

Daily Memory Verse:
Our last Bible memory verse! You've done such a GREAT job over the last 14 days. Let's lock this last memory verse into our jam packed memory banks! Let's say it out loud 5 times as loud as we can!
James 1:22
Do not merely listen to the Word, and so deceive yourselves.
Do what it says.

Activity:
For our final devotional activity let's play bee-atitude charades! Let's try to act out each beatitude and after you've called out each one, share examples of how you can live them out in everyday life.

We're so thankful you've joined us for this mini-devotional on the Beatitudes. Be sure to check out the other mini-devotionals we have available for you and stay tuned for more to come!

May the Lord bless you and keep you and make His face shine upon you every single day!

Blessings, friends!

www.ingramcontent.com/pod-product-compliance
Lightning Source LLC
Chambersburg PA
CBHW071506070426
42452CB00041B/2479